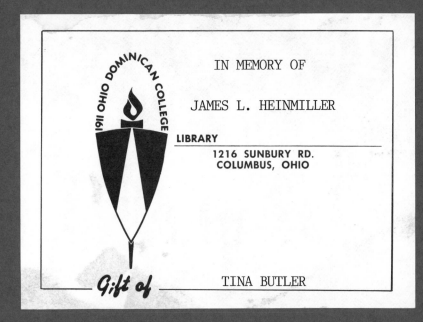

My Father

WORDS AND MUSIC BY JUDY COLLINS
PICTURES BY JANE DYER

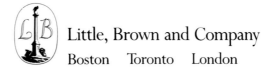

Little, Brown and Company
Boston Toronto London

First edition

Library of Congress Cataloging-in-Publication Data

Collins, Judy, 1939–
    My father/words and music by Judy Collins; pictures by Jane Dyer.
        p.   cm.
    Summary: A shared dream carries family members out of their drab life
into a finer world of music and travel, a dream later fulfilled by the youngest
daughter when she becomes a parent herself.
    ISBN 0-316-15228-5
    1. Children's songs — United States. [1. Family life — Songs and music.
2. Parent and child — Songs and music. 3. Songs.] I. Dyer, Jane, ill. II. Title.
PZ8.3.C683My 1989
784.6′2405 — dc19   88-13945
                                                              CIP
                                                               AC

10 9 8 7 6 5 4 3 2 1

WOR

Published simultaneously in Canada
by Little, Brown & Company (Canada) Limited

Printed in the United States of America

*Paintings done in Luma dyes and colored pencils on 140-pound
Fabriano watercolor paper*

Calligraphy by Jeanyee Wong

My Father was written many years ago
and although my father never heard
the song, I have always felt that
the lyric made a spiritual connection
between my father and myself.

J.C.

For my father,
who shared his dreams.

J.D.

My Father

WORDS AND MUSIC BY JUDY COLLINS

Lyrically, nostalgic

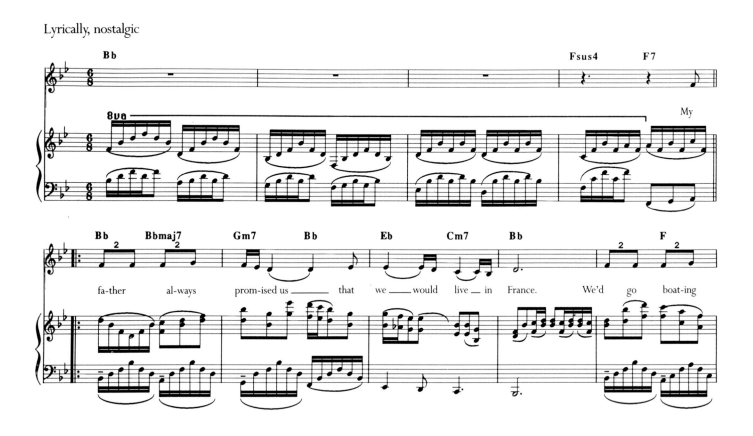

fa-ther al-ways prom-ised us ____ that we ____ would live __ in France. We'd go boat-ing

My father always promised us that we would live in France.

We'd go boating on the Seine

And I would learn to dance.

We lived in Ohio then;

He worked in the mines.

On his streams like boats we knew we'd sail in time.

All my sisters soon were gone to Denver and Cheyenne,

Marrying their grownup dreams, the lilacs and the man.

I stayed behind the youngest still, only danced alone,

The colors of my father's dreams faded without a sigh.

And I live in Paris now, my children dance and dream

Hearing the ways of a miner's life in words they've never seen.